cookie *gifts*

cookie
gifts

Lavish treats to make at home

MOLLY PERHAM

LORENZ BOOKS

First published in 2000 by Lorenz Books

© Anness Publishing Limited 2000

Lorenz Books is an imprint of
Anness Publishing Limited,
Hermes House,
88–89 Blackfriars Road,
London SE1 8HA

Published in the USA by Lorenz Books,
Anness Publishing Inc., 27 West 20th Street,
New York, NY 10011; (800) 354-9657

This edition published in Canada by Raincoast Books
8680 Cambie Street
Vancouver
British Columbia V6P 6M9

A CIP catalogue record for this book is available from
the British Library

Publisher **Joanna Lorenz**
Project editor **Sarah Ainley**
Designer **Jane Coney**
Jacket photography **Peter Cassidy**
Photography **Karl Adamson, Edward Allwright, Steve Baxter,
Peter Cassidy, James Duncan, John Freeman,
Michelle Garrett, Polly Wreford**
Recipes **Jacqueline Clark, Joanna Farrow, Christine France,
Elisabeth Lambert Ortiz, Gilly Love, Sallie Morris,
Pamela Westland, Elizabeth Wolf-Cohen**
Indexer **Helen Snaith**

1 3 5 7 9 10 8 6 4 2

contents

introduction

Home-made cookies make charming gifts.

Not only do they taste irresistible, but if you

gift-wrap them with thought and flair, they will

look fantastic too. This collection of recipes

includes cookies for everyone and every

occasion, so choose a recipe to fit a theme,

a season, or simply to treat someone special

to a favourite indulgence.

storing *cookies*

Cookies should always be cooled completely before storing. When stored for any length of time, crisp cookies go soft, and soft ones will dry out and harden: the key is to make sure your chosen container is completely airtight. A jar or tin with a tight-fitting lid is ideal, or choose a rigid, plastic lidded box. If you want to be absolutely sure your cookies will store well, pack them first in a sealed plastic bag, or cover the top of the container with clear film (plastic wrap) before fitting the lid.

GLASS JARS

Sturdy jars with airtight stoppers or corks, or screw-topped lids, allow the cookies to be seen. Choose jars in novelty shapes and colours to make your gift look extra special.

TINS

Sealable tins make great airtight containers for cookies and come in all shapes and sizes. Look for interesting designs in kitchen shops and stationers, or revamp old food tins for a personal touch.

gift-wrapping *cookies*

For a perfect present, the wrapping of your cookie gifts can be made as special as the contents.

NOVEL ACCESSORIES

Look out for attractive accessories with which to enhance packaging. Many shops now specialize in decorative embellishments, or make your own gilded fruits, flowerheads or pine cones. Keep a selection to hand to mix and match for your cookie gifts.

GIFT CARDS AND TAGS

These can be chosen to co-ordinate with your paper, box or container. Make your own tags by sticking your chosen paper on to a small piece of card, punching a hole in the corner and adding ribbon: even a single ribbon will transform a gift.

GIFT-WRAPPING MATERIALS

The emphasis on gift-wrap has increased considerably in recent years but it is not difficult to package gifts beautifully at home, using any number of different materials. Keep an eye open for stylized bags and boxes in antique shops and markets, and choose containers made from unusual materials such as fabric, plastic, tin, painted glass or crafted wood.

GIFT BOXES

These make wonderful containers for cookies, and you will find an endless supply of designs, colours and sizes in stationers and department stores. If the cookies are to be given (and eaten) quickly, rather than stored, a pretty box lined with tissue paper is ideal.

DECORATIVE BAGS

Paper and fabric bags can be used to pack cookies, although they are not suitable for cookies that will be stored for more than a week. Even the most utilitarian brown paper bag is transformed when sprayed with gold and silver paint. For an exquisite finishing touch, wire luxury chocolates to ribbon, or go minimal and wrap your cookies in clear cellophane, tied up with a length of string.

traditional *cookies*

Scottish *shortbread*

Old-fashioned shortbread looks even more traditional when shaped in a mould and patterned with a thistle motif.

MAKES 2 SHORTBREADS

175G/6OZ/1½ CUPS PLAIN (ALL-PURPOSE) FLOUR

50G/2OZ/½ CUP CORNFLOUR (CORNSTARCH)

50G/2OZ/¼ CUP SUGAR, PLUS EXTRA FOR SPRINKLING

115G/4OZ/½ CUP UNSALTED BUTTER, CHOPPED

1 Preheat the oven to 160°C/325°F/Gas 3. Flour the mould and line one or two baking sheets with non-stick baking paper (parchment).

2 Sift the flour, cornflour (cornstarch) and sugar into bowl. Rub the butter into the flour mixture until you can knead it into a dough.

3 Place half the dough into the mould and press to fit neatly. Invert the mould on to the baking sheet and tap to release the shape. Repeat with the remaining dough. Bake for 35–40 minutes, until pale golden in colour.

4 Sprinkle the top of each shortbread with sugar and leave to cool on the baking sheet. Pack the shortbreads in a box tied with a tartan (plaid) ribbon to complete the gift.

chocolate chip oat *cookies*

12 ● traditional *cookies*

MAKES 60

115G/4OZ/1 CUP PLAIN
    (ALL-PURPOSE) FLOUR
2.5ML/½ TSP BICARBONATE
    OF SODA (BAKING SODA)
1.5ML/¼ TSP BAKING POWDER
PINCH OF SALT
115G/4OZ/½ CUP BUTTER
115G/4OZ/½ CUP CASTER
    (SUPERFINE) SUGAR
90G/3½OZ/SCANT ½ CUP
    LIGHT BROWN SUGAR
1 EGG
2.5ML/½ TSP VANILLA
    ESSENCE (EXTRACT)
75G/3OZ/¾ CUP ROLLED OATS
175G/6OZ/1 CUP CHOCOLATE
    CHIPS

1 Preheat the oven to 180°C/350°F/Gas 4. Grease 3–4 baking sheets. Sift the flour, bicarbonate of soda (baking soda), baking powder and salt into a mixing bowl.

2 Cream together the butter and the two sugars. Add the egg and vanilla essence (extract) and beat until light and fluffy. Beat in the flour mixture until blended.

3 Stir in the oats and chocolate chips. The dough should be crumbly. Drop teaspoonfuls of the dough on to the baking sheets, spacing the cookies so that they can spread.

4 Bake for 15 minutes until firm around the edge but soft to the touch in the centre. Transfer the cookies to a wire rack and allow to cool completely before wrapping as a gift.

melting *moments*

These ever-popular cookies are very crisp and light – and as their name suggests, they really do melt in your mouth.

MAKES 16–20

40G/1½OZ/3 TBSP BUTTER

65G/2½OZ/5 TBSP LARD

75G/3OZ/SCANT ½ CUP
　　SUGAR

½ EGG, BEATEN

FEW DROPS OF VANILLA OR
　　ALMOND ESSENCE (EXTRACT)

150G/5OZ/1¼ CUPS
　　SELF-RAISING
　　(SELF-RISING) FLOUR

ROLLED OATS, FOR COATING

4–5 GLACÉ (CANDIED)
　　CHERRIES, QUARTERED

1 Preheat the oven to 180°C/350°F/Gas 4. Grease two baking sheets. Cream together the butter, lard and sugar, then gradually beat in the egg and vanilla or almond essence (extract).

2 Stir the flour into the beaten mixture, then roll into 16–20 small balls in your hands.

3 Spread the rolled oats over a sheet of greaseproof (waxed) paper. Roll the balls in the oats so that they are coated evenly all over.

4 Place the balls, well spaced, on the baking sheets, place a piece of cherry on top of each and bake for 15 minutes, until golden.

Italian *biscotti*

These sophisticated Italian cookies are part-baked, sliced to reveal a feast of mixed nuts and then baked again until crisp and golden. Traditionally they are served dipped in *vin santo*, a sweet dessert wine.

MAKES 24

50G/2OZ/¼ CUP UNSALTED

BUTTER

115G/4OZ/GENEROUS ½ CUP

SUGAR

175G/6OZ/1½ CUPS

SELF-RAISING

(SELF-RISING) FLOUR

PINCH OF SALT

10ML/2 TSP BAKING POWDER

5ML/1 TSP GROUND

CORIANDER

FINELY GRATED ZEST

OF 1 LEMON

50G/2OZ/½ CUP POLENTA

1 EGG, LIGHTLY BEATEN

10ML/2 TSP BRANDY OR

ORANGE-FLAVOURED

LIQUEUR

50G/2OZ/½ CUP

UNBLANCHED ALMONDS

50G/2OZ/½ CUP PISTACHIO

NUTS

1 Preheat the oven to 160°C/325°F/Gas 3. Grease a baking sheet.

2 Cream the butter and sugar. Sift the flour, salt, baking powder and coriander into a bowl. Add lemon zest, polenta, egg and brandy or liqueur and mix to a soft dough. Stir in the pistachio nuts.

3 Halve, then shape each half into a flat loaf. Bake for 30 minutes until risen and firm.

4 Remove from the oven. When cool, cut each loaf diagonally into 12 slices, then cook for a further 10 minutes, until crisp. Allow to cool. Store in an airtight container for up to one week.

COOK'S TIP

Use a sharp, serrated knife, to slice the cooled cookies, or they will crumble.

chocolate *kisses*

These rich little cookies would look particularly tempting mixed together in a decorative box. They make the perfect accompaniment to scoops of chocolate ice cream.

MAKES 24

75G/3OZ PLAIN (SEMISWEET) CHOCOLATE, CHOPPED

75G/3OZ WHITE CHOCOLATE, CHOPPED

115G/4OZ/½ CUP BUTTER

115G/4OZ/GENEROUS ½ CUP CASTER (SUPERFINE) SUGAR

2 EGGS

225G/8OZ/2 CUPS PLAIN (ALL-PURPOSE) FLOUR

ICING (CONFECTIONER'S) SUGAR, TO DECORATE

1 Melt each chocolate in a heatproof bowl over a pan of hot water. Set aside to cool. Cream the butter and sugar until pale and fluffy. Beat in the eggs, one at a time, sift in the flour and mix well.

2 Halve the cookie mixture and divide it evenly between the two bowls of melted chocolate. Mix each chocolate in well until blended.

3 Knead both the doughs until smooth and elastic, then wrap in clear film (plastic wrap) and chill for 1 hour. Meanwhile, preheat the oven to 190°C/375°F/ Gas 5. Grease two baking sheets and set aside.

4 Roll teaspoonfuls of both doughs into balls and arrange on the baking sheets. Bake for 10 minutes, dust with icing (confectioner's) sugar and allow to cool.

macaroons

Freshly ground almonds, lightly toasted beforehand to intensify the flavour, give these cookies their rich taste and texture. For best results, avoid using ready-ground almonds as a shortcut.

MAKES 12

115G/4OZ/½ CUP BLANCHED
   ALMONDS, TOASTED
165G/5½OZ/GENEROUS ¾ CUP
   CASTER (SUPERFINE) SUGAR
2 EGG WHITES
2.5ML/½ TSP ALMOND
   ESSENCE (EXTRACT)
ICING (CONFECTIONER'S)
   SUGAR, FOR DUSTING

1 Preheat the oven to 180°C/350°F/Gas 4. Line a baking sheet with baking paper (parchment).

2 Reserve 12 almonds for decorating. In a food processor, grind the remaining almonds with the sugar. Pour in the egg whites and add the almond essence (extract).

3 With moistened hands, roll the cookie mixture into walnut-size balls and arrange on the prepared baking sheet. Press one of the reserved almonds on to each ball.

4 Flatten the balls slightly and dust with icing (confectioner's) sugar. Bake for 10 minutes, until the tops feel firm. Cool slightly, then peel the cookies off the paper and leave to cool completely.

COOK'S TIP

To toast the almonds, spread them on a baking sheet and bake in the preheated oven for about 10 minutes, until golden. Leave to cool completely before grinding.

madeleines

These tea cakes, baked in a special pan with individual shell-shaped cups, were made famous by French author Marcel Proust, who starts one of his novels with the taste of a madeleine. They are best eaten on the day they are made.

MAKES 12

165G/5½OZ/GENEROUS
    1¼ CUPS PLAIN
    (ALL-PURPOSE) FLOUR
5ML/1 TSP BAKING POWDER
2 EGGS
75G/3OZ/¾ CUP ICING
    (CONFECTIONER'S) SUGAR,
    PLUS EXTRA FOR DUSTING
GRATED ZEST OF 1 LEMON
15ML/1 TBSP LEMON OR
    ORANGE JUICE
75G/3OZ/6 TBSP UNSALTED
    BUTTER, MELTED AND
    SLIGHTLY COOLED

1 Preheat the oven to 190°C/375°F/Gas 5. Butter a 12-cup madeleine pan. Sift together the flour and baking powder.

2 Using an electric mixer, beat the eggs and icing (confectioner's) sugar for 5 minutes until thick and creamy and the mixture forms a ribbon when the beaters are lifted. Gently fold in the lemon zest and juice.

3 Beginning with the flour, alternately fold in the flour and the melted butter in four batches.

4 Leave the mixture to stand for 10 minutes, then carefully spoon into the tin. Tap the side of the tin very gently to release any air bubbles.

5 Bake for 12 minutes, rotating the tin halfway through cooking, until a skewer inserted in the centre comes out clean. Turn on to a wire rack to cool completely and dust with icing sugar before serving.

COOK'S TIP

If you don't have a pan for making madeleines, use a muffin tin, preferably one with a non-stick coating. The cakes won't have the ridges and shell shape, but they do look pretty dusted with a little icing sugar.

Mexican almond *cookies*

For a gift with a taste of balmy summer heat, give these almond-flavoured cookies – an old Mexican favourite.

MAKES 24

115G/4OZ/1 CUP PLAIN
  (ALL-PURPOSE) FLOUR
175G/6OZ/1½ CUPS ICING
  (CONFECTIONER'S) SUGAR
PINCH OF SALT
50G/2OZ/½ CUP ALMONDS,
  FINELY CHOPPED
2.5ML/½ TSP VANILLA ESSENCE
  (EXTRACT)
115G/4OZ/½ CUP
  UNSALTED BUTTER
ICING SUGAR, FOR DUSTING

1 Preheat the oven to 180°C/350°F/Gas 4. Grease two baking sheets.

2 Sift the flour, icing (confectioner's) sugar and salt into a mixing bowl. Add the almonds and stir well to combine.

3 Add the vanilla essence (extract). Using your fingertips, work in the butter to make a dough.

4 Form the dough into a ball and roll out on a floured surface until 3mm/⅛in thick. With a fluted cutter, make about 24 cookies.

5 Transfer the cookies to baking sheets and bake for 30 minutes.

6 Transfer the cookies to wire racks to cool, then dust thickly with icing sugar.

VARIATION

Try using other nuts such as walnuts, peanuts or pecans for a change.

lavender heart *cookies*

In traditional folklore, lavender and hearts have both been linked with love, so make some heart-shaped cookies as a gift for St Valentine's Day or a romantic anniversary.

MAKES 16–18

115G/4oz/½ CUP
UNSALTED BUTTER

50G/2oz/¼ CUP SUGAR

175G/6oz/1½ CUPS PLAIN
(ALL-PURPOSE) FLOUR

30ML/2 TBSP FRESH
LAVENDER FLORETS OR
15ML/1 TBSP DRIED
CULINARY LAVENDER,
ROUGHLY CHOPPED

30ML/2 TBSP SUGAR, FOR
SPRINKLING

1 Cream the butter and sugar in a large bowl until fluffy. Stir in the flour and lavender and, using your fingertips, form into a soft ball. Cover with clear film (plastic wrap) and chill for 15 minutes.

2 Preheat the oven to 200°C/400°F/Gas 6. Roll out the dough on a floured work surface and stamp out 18 cookies, using a floured 5cm/2in heart-shaped cutter.

3 Place the cookie shapes on a greased baking sheet and bake for 10 minutes, until golden.

4 Sprinkle the cookies with sugar. Leave them to stand for about 5 minutes before transferring from the baking sheet to a wire rack to cool completely. Store in an airtight container for up to one week.

old-fashioned ginger *cookies*

MAKES 60

300G/11OZ/2⅔ CUPS PLAIN
(ALL-PURPOSE) FLOUR

5ML/1 TSP BICARBONATE
OF SODA (BAKING SODA)

7.5ML/1½ TSP GROUND
GINGER

1.5ML/¼ TSP GROUND
CINNAMON

1.5ML/¼ TSP GROUND CLOVES

115G/4OZ/½ CUP BUTTER

350G/12OZ/1¾ CUPS
SUGAR

1 EGG, BEATEN

60ML/4 TBSP BLACK TREACLE
(MOLASSES)

5ML/1 TSP LEMON JUICE

1 Preheat the oven to 160°C/325°F/Gas 3. Grease 3–4 baking trays.

2 Sift the flour, bicarbonate of soda (baking soda) and spices into a mixing bowl.

3 Cream together the butter and two-thirds of the sugar. Stir in the egg, treacle (molasses) and lemon juice. Add the flour mixture and mix with a wooden spoon to make a soft dough.

4 Shape the dough into 2cm/¾in balls. Roll the balls in the remaining sugar and place them about 5cm/2in apart on the prepared baking trays, so that the cookies have plenty of room to spread.

5 Bake for about 12 minutes until the cookies are firm.

6 With a slotted spatula, transfer the cookies to a wire rack and leave to cool.

Easter *cookies*

These lightly-spiced biscuits are enjoyed throughout the Christian world as a traditional part of the Easter festival.

MAKES 16–18

115G/4OZ/½ CUP UNSALTED BUTTER, CHOPPED

75G/3OZ/SCANT ½ CUP SUGAR, PLUS EXTRA FOR SPRINKLING

1 EGG, SEPARATED

200G/7OZ/1⅔ CUPS PLAIN (ALL-PURPOSE) FLOUR

2.5ML/½ TSP GROUND MIXED SPICE (ALL-SPICE)

2.5ML/½ TSP GROUND CINNAMON

50G/2OZ/¼ CUP CURRANTS

15ML/1 TBSP CHOPPED MIXED (CANDIED CITRUS) PEEL

15–30ML/1–2 TBSP MILK

1 Preheat the oven to 200°C/400°F/Gas 6. Grease two baking sheets and set them aside.

2 Beat together the butter and sugar until light and fluffy, then beat in the egg yolk.

3 Sift the flour and spices over the egg mixture, then fold in with the currants and peel, adding sufficient milk to mix to a soft dough.

4 Turn the dough on to a floured surface, knead until smooth, then roll out using a floured rolling pin, to 5mm/¼in thick. Cut the dough into rounds using a 5cm/2in fluted cookie cutter.

5 Transfer to the prepared baking sheets and bake for 10 minutes.

6 Beat the egg white, then brush over the cookies. Sprinkle with sugar and bake for a further 10 minutes, until golden. Leave to cool.

chocolate *dreams*

chocolate *amaretti*

MAKES 24

150G/5OZ/1¼ CUPS BLANCHED
   WHOLE ALMONDS

90G/3½OZ/½ CUP CASTER
   (SUPERFINE) SUGAR

15ML/1 TBSP COCOA POWDER

30ML/2 TBSP ICING
   (CONFECTIONER'S) SUGAR

2 EGG WHITES

PINCH OF CREAM OF TARTAR

5ML/1 TSP ALMOND ESSENCE
   (EXTRACT)

FLAKED (SLIVERED) ALMONDS,
   TO DECORATE

1 Preheat the oven to 180°C/350°F/ Gas 4. Place the almonds on a baking sheet and bake for 10–12 minutes until golden brown. Leave to cool. Reduce the oven temperature to 160°C/ 325°F/Gas 3. Line a large baking sheet with baking paper (parchment).

2 In a food processor, process the almonds with half the caster (superfine) sugar until finely ground but not oily. Transfer to a bowl and sift in the cocoa and icing (confectioner's) sugar. Set aside.

3 Beat the egg whites and cream of tartar until stiff peaks form. Sprinkle in the remaining caster sugar a tablespoon at a time, beating well, until the egg whites are stiff and glossy. Beat in the almond essence (extract).

4 Sprinkle over the cocoa mixture and fold into the egg whites. Spoon into a piping bag fitted with a plain 1cm/⅜in nozzle. Pipe 4cm/1½in rounds about 2.5cm/1in apart on the baking sheet. Press an almond into each.

5 Bake the cookies for 12 minutes until crisp to the touch. Allow the cookies to cool on the baking sheet for 10 minutes, then transfer them to a wire rack to cool completely. Pack into a glass jar with an airtight stopper.

chocolate fruit and nut *cookies*

These simple, chunky cookies are made using the spiced German gingerbread, Lebkuchen, as a base. The combination of walnuts, almonds and cherries is very effective, but you can use any mixture of candied fruits and nuts.

MAKES 20

50G/2OZ/¼ CUP CASTER
  (SUPERFINE) SUGAR
75ML/3FL OZ/⅓ CUP WATER
225G/8OZ PLAIN (SEMISWEET)
  CHOCOLATE, CHOPPED
40G/1½OZ/½ CUP WALNUT
  HALVES
75G/3OZ/⅓ CUP GLACÉ
  (CANDIED) CHERRIES,
  CHOPPED
115G/4OZ/1 CUP WHOLE
  BLANCHED ALMONDS

FOR THE LEBKUCHEN

115G/4OZ/½ CUP BUTTER
115G/4OZ/½ CUP LIGHT
  BROWN SUGAR
1 EGG, BEATEN
115G/4OZ/⅓ CUP BLACK
  TREACLE (MOLASSES)
400G/14OZ/3½ CUPS
  SELF-RAISING (SELF-RISING)
  FLOUR

5ML/1 TSP GROUND GINGER
2.5ML/½ TSP GROUND CLOVES
1.5ML/¼ TSP CHILLI POWDER

1 For the Lebkuchen, cream together the butter and sugar until pale and fluffy. Beat in the egg and black treacle (molasses). Sift the flour, ginger, cloves and chilli powder into the bowl. Mix the ingredients together to make a stiff paste. Turn on to a floured work surface and knead lightly until smooth. Wrap and chill for 30 minutes.

2 Preheat the oven to 180°C/350°F/Gas 4. Grease two baking sheets and them set aside.

3 Shape the dough into a roll 20cm/8in long. Chill for 30 minutes. Cut into 20 slices and space them on the baking sheets. Bake for about 10 minutes. Leave the slices on the baking sheets for 5 minutes, then transfer to a wire rack to cool.

4 Meanwhile, put the caster (superfine) sugar and water in a saucepan. Heat gently, until the sugar dissolves. Bring to the boil.

5 Boil for 1 minute, until syrupy. Cool, and then gradually stir in the chocolate until it has made a smooth sauce.

6 Place the wire rack over a large tray or board. Spoon a little of the chocolate mixture over each cookie, spreading it to the edges. Press a walnut half into the centre of each. Arrange pieces of glacé (candied) cherry and almonds around the nuts. Leave to set in a cool place.

chocolate nut *clusters*

These novelty cookies are ideal for eating at the end of a dinner party, and would make the perfect surprise gift for the host.

MAKES 30

550ML/18FL OZ/2½ CUPS
    DOUBLE (HEAVY) CREAM
25G/1OZ/2 TBSP UNSALTED
    BUTTER, CHOPPED
350ML/12FL OZ/1½ CUPS
    GOLDEN (LIGHT CORN)
    SYRUP
200G/7OZ/1 CUP CASTER
    (SUPERFINE) SUGAR
90G/3½OZ/SCANT ½ CUP
    LIGHT BROWN SUGAR
PINCH OF SALT
15ML/1 TBSP VANILLA
    ESSENCE (EXTRACT)
425G/15OZ/3¾ CUPS
    HAZELNUTS, PECANS,
    WALNUTS, BRAZIL NUTS
    OR UNSALTED PEANUTS,
400G/14OZ PLAIN (SEMISWEET)
    CHOCOLATE, CHOPPED
25G/1OZ/2 TBSP WHITE
    VEGETABLE FAT
    (SHORTENING)

1 Lightly oil two baking sheets. In a heavy-based saucepan over a medium heat, cook the first six ingredients until the sugars dissolve and the butter melts.

2 Bring to the boil and cook, stirring frequently, for 1 minute, until the caramel reaches 119°C/238°F (soft ball stage) on a sugar thermometer. Place the bottom of the saucepan in a bowl of cold water to stop cooking.

3 Cool slightly, then stir in the vanilla essence (extract). Stir the nuts into the caramel until coated. Using an oiled tablespoon, drop spoonfuls of the nut mixture on to the prepared sheets, about 2.5cm/1in apart. If the mixture hardens, return the pan to the heat to soften.

4 Refrigerate the clusters for about 30 minutes, until they are firm and cold, or leave them in a cool place until they have hardened.

5 Using a palette knife (spatula), transfer the clusters to a wire rack placed over a baking sheet.

6 Melt the chocolate and white vegetable fat (shortening) in a pan, over a low heat, stirring until smooth. Cool slightly, then spoon the chocolate over each cluster.

chocolate dreams • 26

7 Alternatively, using a fork, dip each cluster into chocolate and lift out, tapping on the edge of the saucepan to shake off any excess.

8 Place on the wire rack over the baking sheet. Allow to set for 2 hours, until hardened.

COOK'S TIP

If you do not possess a sugar thermometer, you can test cooked sugar for soft ball stage by spooning a small amount into a bowl of cold water; when taken out it should form a soft ball when rolled between finger and thumb.

decorated chocolate *Lebkuchen*

Wrapped in paper or cellophane, or beautifully boxed, these decorated gingerbread cookies make a lovely present. Don't make them too far in advance as the chocolate will gradually discolour.

MAKES 40

1 QUANTITY LEBKUCHEN
   MIXTURE (SEE PAGE 24)

115G/4OZ PLAIN (SEMISWEET)
   CHOCOLATE, CHOPPED

115G/4OZ MILK CHOCOLATE,
   CHOPPED

115G/4OZ WHITE
   CHOCOLATE, CHOPPED

CHOCOLATE VERMICELLI
   (SPRINKLES), FOR
   SPRINKLING

COCOA POWDER, FOR
   DUSTING

1 Grease two baking sheets. Roll out half the Lebkuchen mixture and cut 20 heart shapes. Gather the remaining dough and cut into 20 pieces. Roll into balls, place on the baking sheets and flatten each ball.

2 Chill both sheets of dough shapes for 30 minutes. Preheat the oven to 180°C/350°F/ Gas 4 and bake for 8–10 minutes. Leave to cool on a wire rack.

3 Melt the plain (semisweet) chocolate in a heatproof bowl over hot water. Melt the milk and white chocolate in separate bowls.

4 Make three paper piping bags using greaseproof (waxed) paper. Spoon a little of each different chocolate into each of the three paper piping bags and set aside until needed.

5 Spoon a little plain chocolate over one third of the cookies, spreading it to cover them completely.

6 Snip the tip off the bag of white chocolate and drizzle it over some of the coated cookies, to decorate.

7 Sprinkle chocolate vermicelli (sprinkles) over the undecorated cookies. Coat the remaining cookies with milk and white chocolate and decorate some of these with more chocolate from the piping bags, contrasting the colours. Scatter more cookies with vermicelli. Leave to set.

8 Transfer the undecorated cookies to a plate or tray and dust lightly with cocoa powder.

chocolate hazelnut *crescents*

Chocolate and nuts together are irresistible. Walnuts or pecans can be used instead of hazelnuts, if finely chopped.

MAKES 35

300G/11OZ/2⅔ CUPS PLAIN
    (ALL-PURPOSE) FLOUR

PINCH OF SALT

225G/8OZ/1 CUP UNSALTED
    BUTTER

50G/2OZ/¼ CUP CASTER
    (SUPERFINE) SUGAR

15ML/1 TBSP HAZELNUT
    LIQUEUR OR WATER

5ML/1 TSP VANILLA ESSENCE
    (EXTRACT)

75G/3OZ PLAIN (SEMISWEET)
    CHOCOLATE, GRATED

65G/2½OZ/½ CUP HAZEL-
    NUTS, TOASTED AND
    FINELY CHOPPED

ICING (CONFECTIONER'S)
    SUGAR, FOR DUSTING

350G/12OZ PLAIN
    (SEMISWEET) CHOCOLATE,
    MELTED, FOR DIPPING

1 Preheat the oven to 160°C/325°F/Gas 3. Grease two baking sheets. Sift the flour and salt into a bowl and set aside.

2 Beat the butter and sugar with the liqueur or water and the vanilla essence (extract). Stir in the flour, then fold in the chocolate and nuts.

3 Shape the dough into crescent shapes. Place on the baking sheets and bake for 20 minutes.

4 Allow the cookies to cool on the baking sheets for 10 minutes, then transfer the cookies from the baking sheets to wire racks to cool completely. Line the baking sheets with baking paper (parchment). Dust the cookies with icing (confectioner's) sugar.

5 Dip half of each crescent into melted chocolate, then place on the prepared baking sheets. Chill until set.

chunky pecan chocolate *drops*

Do not allow these cookies to cool completely on the baking sheet or they will become too crisp and will break when you try to lift them.

MAKES 18

175G/6OZ PLAIN
   (SEMISWEET) CHOCOLATE,
   CHOPPED

115G/4OZ/½ CUP UNSALTED
   BUTTER, CHOPPED

2 EGGS

90G/3½OZ/½ CUP CASTER
   (SUPERFINE) SUGAR

50G/2OZ/¼ CUP LIGHT
   BROWN SUGAR

40G/1½OZ/⅓ CUP PLAIN
   (ALL-PURPOSE) FLOUR

25G/1OZ/¼ CUP COCOA
   POWDER

5ML/1 TSP BAKING POWDER

10ML/2 TSP VANILLA ESSENCE
   (EXTRACT)

PINCH OF SALT

115G/4OZ/1 CUP PECANS,
   TOASTED AND COARSELY
   CHOPPED

175G/6OZ/1 CUP
   CHOCOLATE CHIPS

115G/4OZ FINE QUALITY
   WHITE CHOCOLATE, IN
   5MM/¼IN PIECES

115G/4OZ FINE QUALITY
   MILK CHOCOLATE, IN
   5MM/¼IN PIECES

1 Preheat the oven to 160°C/325°F/Gas 3. Grease two baking sheets. In a heatproof bowl over hot water, melt the plain (semisweet) chocolate and butter. Remove from the heat and set aside to cool.

2 Using an electric mixer, beat the eggs and sugars for about 2 minutes, until creamy.

3 Pour in the melted chocolate mixture, beating until well blended. Beat in the flour, cocoa powder, baking powder, vanilla essence (extract) and salt. Stir in the nuts and remaining chocolate.

4 Drop tablespoonfuls of mixture on to the baking sheets. Bake for 8–10 minutes, until crisp. Remove the baking sheets to a wire rack to cool for 2 minutes, then transfer the cookies to a wire rack.

cookies for *kids*

peanut butter *cookies*

Packing up a picnic? Got a birthday party planned? Make sure these nutty cookies are on the menu!

MAKES 25

30ML/2 TBSP SMOOTH
  PEANUT BUTTER

225G/8OZ/1 CUP BUTTER

115G/4OZ/1 CUP ICING
  (CONFECTIONER'S) SUGAR

50G/2OZ/½ CUP CORNFLOUR
  (CORNSTARCH)

225G/8OZ/2 CUPS PLAIN
  (ALL-PURPOSE) FLOUR

115G/4OZ/1 CUP UNSALTED
  PEANUTS

2 Preheat the oven to 180°C/350°F/Gas 4. Lightly oil two baking sheets. Roll the mixture into 25 small balls and place on the baking sheets.

1 Beat the peanut butter and butter together. Mix in the icing (confectioner's) sugar and flours.

3 Press the tops of the balls of dough flat, using either the back of a fork or your fingertips.

4 Press a few peanuts into each cookie. Bake for 15–20 minutes, until lightly browned.

5 Leave to cool for a few minutes before lifting them on to a wire rack to cool completely.

COOK'S TIP

Make monster cookies by rolling bigger balls of dough. Leave plenty of room for them to spread.

cookies for *kids* ● 33

animal *magic*

Snappy cookies in animal shapes, which can be decorated in your own style.

MAKES 14

175G/6OZ/1½ CUPS SELF-
RAISING (SELF-RISING) FLOUR

2.5ML/½ TSP BICARBONATE
OF SODA (BAKING SODA)

2.5ML/½ TSP GROUND
CINNAMON

10ML/2 TSP CASTER
(SUPERFINE) SUGAR

50G/2OZ/¼ CUP BUTTER

45ML/3 TBSP GOLDEN
(LIGHT CORN) SYRUP

50G/2OZ/½ CUP ICING
(CONFECTIONER'S) SUGAR

5–10ML/1–2 TSP WATER

1 Preheat the oven to 190°C/375°F/Gas 5. Grease two baking sheets.

2 Mix the flour, bicarbonate of soda, (baking soda) cinnamon and sugar in a bowl.

3 Melt the butter and syrup in a saucepan and pour over the dry ingredients in the bowl. Mix together well and then use your hands to pull the mixture together to make a soft dough.

4 Turn on to a floured surface and roll out to about 5mm/¼in thick.

5 Use floured animal cutters to cut shapes from the dough and arrange on the prepared baking sheets, leaving enough room between them to spread.

6 Press the trimmings back into a ball, roll it out and cut more shapes. Continue until all the dough is used. Bake for 8–12 minutes, until lightly browned. Leave to cool slightly, before transferring to a wire rack to cool completely.

7 Sift the icing sugar into a bowl and add enough water to make a fairly soft icing. Spoon the icing into a piping bag fitted with a small, plain nozzle and pipe your own decorations on the cookies.

COOK'S TIP

Any cutters can be used with the same mixture. Obviously, the smaller the cutters, the more biscuits you will make.

jewelled *elephants*

These stunningly robed elephants make a lovely gift for animal-lovers, or an edible decoration for a special occasion. If you make holes in them before baking, you could use them as original Christmas tree decorations.

MAKES 10

1 QUANTITY LEBKUCHEN
   MIXTURE (SEE PAGE 24)

90G/3½OZ ROYAL ICING
   (GLAZE)

RED FOOD COLOURING

225G/8OZ READY-TO-ROLL
   SUGAR PASTE

SMALL CANDY-COVERED
   CHOCOLATES

GOLD DRAGEES

1 Preheat the oven to 180°C/350°F/Gas 4. Grease two baking sheets. Draw an elephant on paper to make a template. Roll out the Lebkuchen mixture and use the template to cut out elephant shapes. Place on the baking sheets and bake for 3–5 minutes. Leave to cool.

2 Put a little icing (glaze) in a paper piping bag fitted with a fine nozzle. (Alternatively, you can snip off the tip of the bag.) Set aside.

3 Knead red food colouring into half the sugar paste. Roll a little red sugar paste into ropes and secure them on the feet and tips of the trunk, using the icing in the bag. Shape oval shapes from the sugar paste for the headdress.

4 Roll out the white sugar paste. Cut out circles, using a 6cm/2½in cookie cutter. Secure to the elephants' backs with icing so that the edge of the sugar paste is about 2.5cm/1in above the top of the legs. Trim off the excess paste.

5 Pipe tassels around the edges. Pipe dots of white icing for eyes, the tops of the trunks, around the necks and feet, and at the tops of the tails.

6 Halve the small candy-covered chocolates and press into the sugar paste above the tassels. Decorate the headdress, chocolates and white sugar paste with gold dragées. Leave to harden before packing.

gingerbread *teddy bears*

These endearing little bears, dressed in striped pyjamas, would make a perfect gift for children of any age. If you can't get a large cutter, make smaller teddy bears or use a traditional gingerbread-man cutter.

MAKES 6

75G/3OZ WHITE CHOCOLATE

175G/6OZ READY-TO-ROLL
WHITE SUGAR PASTE

BLUE FOOD COLOURING

25G/1OZ MILK CHOCOLATE

FOR THE GINGERBREAD

175G/6OZ/1½ CUPS PLAIN
(ALL-PURPOSE) FLOUR

1.5ML/¼ TSP BICARBONATE
OF SODA (BAKING SODA)

PINCH OF SALT

5ML/1 TSP GROUND GINGER

5ML/1 TSP GROUND CINNAMON

65G/2½OZ/5 TBSP UNSALTED
BUTTER, CUBED

75G/3OZ/SCANT ½ CUP
CASTER (SUPERFINE) SUGAR

30ML/2 TBSP GOLDEN
(LIGHT CORN) SYRUP

1 EGG YOLK, BEATEN

ICING (CONFECTIONER'S)
SUGAR, FOR DUSTING

1 To make the ginger-bread, sift together the flour, bicarbonate of soda (baking soda), salt and spices into a bowl. Rub the butter into the flour until the mixture resembles fine bread-crumbs.

2 Stir in the sugar, syrup and egg yolk and mix to a firm dough. Knead lightly. Wrap and chill for 30 minutes.

3 Preheat the oven to 180°C/350°F/Gas 4. Grease two baking sheets. Roll out the dough on a floured surface and cut out teddy shapes, using a 13cm/5in cookie cutter.

4 Transfer the teddy bears to the baking sheets. Bake for 10 minutes, until beginning to colour around the edges. Leave on the baking sheets for 3 minutes and then transfer to a wire rack.

5 Break half the white chocolate into pieces and melt in a heatproof bowl over hot water. Put in a paper piping bag and snip off the tip.

6 Make a neat template for the teddy bears' clothes. Draw an outline of the cutter on to plain paper, then draw a simple design for striped pyjamas, or clothes of your choice.

7 Roll out the sugar paste and cut out the clothes. Secure them with the melted chocolate. Add ears, eyes and snouts.

8 Dilute the blue food colouring with water and paint the pyjamas. Melt the remaining chocolates separately and put in separate piping bags and snip off the tips. Use the white chocolate to outline the pyjamas and use the milk chocolate for the faces. Leave to dry.

honey and nut *clusters*

These cookie bars are based on an old Italian recipe. Serve them in squares or fingers, and keep in the fridge until needed. They are delightfully sticky and kids just love them!

115G/4OZ/1 CUP BLANCHED
    ALMONDS
115G/4OZ/1 CUP SHELLED
    HAZELNUTS
WHITES OF 2 EGGS
115G/4OZ/½ CUP HONEY
115G/4OZ/GENEROUS ½ CUP
    SUGAR

1 Preheat the oven to the lowest setting. Line a 20cm/8in square tin with baking paper (parchment).

2 Toast the almonds and hazelnuts on separate baking sheets in the oven for 30 minutes. Rub off the skins with a cloth and chop both types.

3 Whisk the egg whites in a clean, greasefree bowl until stiff peaks form, and stir in the chopped hazelnuts.

4 Put the honey and sugar into a heavy-based pan and bring to the boil. Add the nut mixture and cook for 10 minutes.

5 Turn into the tin and level the top. Cover with another piece of baking paper, put weights on top and chill for 2 days. Cut into 48 pieces and wrap neatly in baking paper and then in your chosen gift-wrap or in a pretty cotton fabric.

chocolate *crackle-tops*

Older children will have fun making these cookies for friends.

MAKES 38

200G/7OZ PLAIN
  (SEMISWEET) CHOCOLATE,
  CHOPPED
90G/3½OZ/7 TBSP UNSALTED
  BUTTER
115G/4OZ/GENEROUS ½ CUP
  CASTER (SUPERFINE) SUGAR
3 EGGS
5ML/1 TSP VANILLA ESSENCE
  (EXTRACT)
215G/7½OZ/SCANT 2 CUPS
  PLAIN (ALL-PURPOSE) FLOUR
25G/1OZ/¼ CUP COCOA
2.5ML/½ TSP BAKING POWDER
PINCH OF SALT
175G/6OZ/1½ CUPS ICING
  (CONFECTIONER'S) SUGAR

1 Melt the chocolate and butter together over a low heat, stirring frequently. Remove from the heat when smooth.

2 Add the caster (superfine) sugar to the chocolate mixture, and stir gently until it dissolves. Add the eggs one at a time, beating well after each addition; stir in the vanilla essence (extract).

3 Sift together the flour, cocoa, baking powder and salt. Stir into the chocolate mixture in batches, until just blended.

4 Cover the dough and refrigerate for at least 1 hour, until the dough is cold and holds its shape.

5 Preheat the oven to 160°C/325°F/Gas 3. Grease three large baking sheets and set aside.

6 Place the icing (confectioner's) sugar in a bowl. Using a teaspoon, take scoops of the dough, and roll it into 4cm/1½in balls with your hands.

7 Dip each ball in icing sugar, then bake for 10 minutes, until the tops feel firm. Cool slightly on the baking sheets, then transfer to a wire rack to cool completely.

candy *necklaces*

This is a delightful idea for a novelty gift. Arrange in a pretty, tissue-lined box for presentation.

MAKES 12

1 QUANTITY GINGERBREAD
 MIXTURE (SEE PAGE 38)
200G/7OZ ROYAL ICING (GLAZE)
PINK FOOD COLOURING
SELECTION OF CANDIES
3M/3 YDS RIBBON

1 Preheat the oven to 180°C/350°F/Gas 4. Grease 2 baking sheets. Roll out just over half the gingerbread to a thickness of 5mm/¼in.

2 Cut out stars using a 2.5cm/1in cutter. Transfer to a baking sheet.

3 Make a large hole in the centre of each of the stars, using a skewer.

4 Gather the trimmings together with the remaining gingerbread dough. Roll the dough in the palm of your hands, to make a sausage shape about 2.5cm/1in in diameter. Cut into 1cm/½in slices. Place the slices on the second baking sheet, making sure they are well spaced apart. Make a hole in the centre of each slice, using a skewer.

5 Bake for 8 minutes, until slightly risen and just beginning to colour. Remove from the oven and, while still warm, re-make the skewer holes, as the gingerbread will have spread during baking. Cool on a wire rack.

6 Put half the royal icing (glaze) in a paper piping bag and snip off the tip. Pipe outlines around the stars. Colour the remaining icing pink. Spoon into a piping bag fitted with a star nozzle.

7 Pipe three stars onto each round cookie. Cut each piece of candy into smaller pieces and use to decorate the cookies. Leave to harden.

8 Cut the ribbon into 50cm/20in lengths. Thread a selection of the cookies on to each ribbon. Line a pretty box with plenty of tissue paper and arrange the candy necklaces inside.

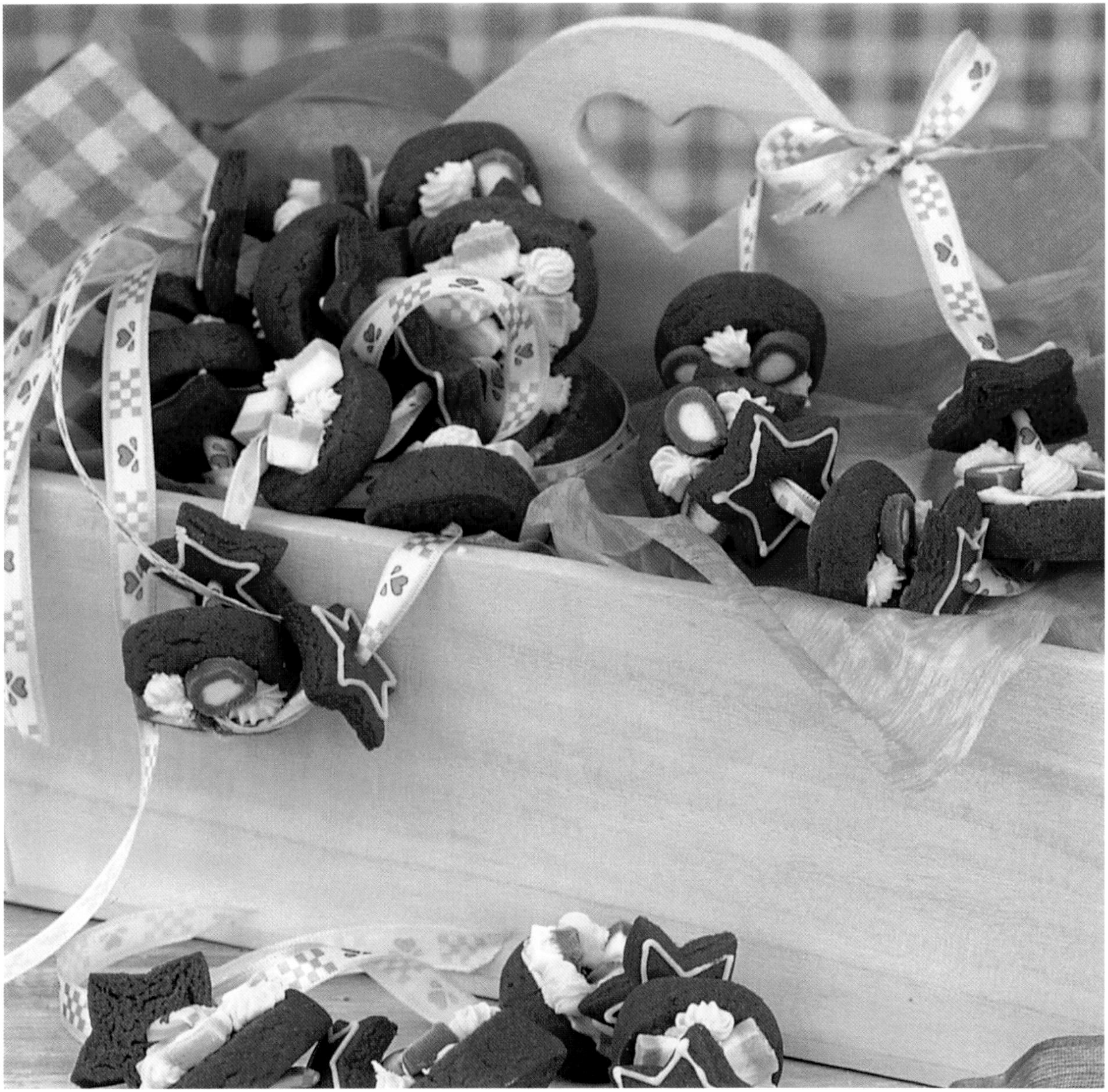

Christmas *cookies*

jewelled Christmas *trees*

These cookies make an appealing gift. They look wonderful on a Christmas tree or in front of a window to catch the light.

MAKES 12

175G/6OZ/1½ CUPS PLAIN
(ALL-PURPOSE) FLOUR

75G/3OZ/⅓ CUP BUTTER,
CHOPPED

40G/1½OZ/3 TBSP SUGAR

1 EGG WHITE

30ML/2 TBSP ORANGE JUICE

225G/8OZ COLOURED
FRUIT CANDY

COLOURED RIBBONS, TO
DECORATE

1 Preheat the oven to 180°C/350°F/Gas 4. Line two baking sheets with non-stick baking paper (parchment). Sift the flour into a mixing bowl. Using your fingertips, rub in the butter until the mixture resembles breadcrumbs.

2 Stir in the sugar, egg white and orange juice to form a soft dough. Knead on a lightly floured surface until smooth.

3 Roll the dough out thinly and stamp out Christmas tree shapes using a floured cutter.

4 Transfer the tree shapes to the prepared baking sheets.

5 Using a 1cm/½in round cutter, stamp out six holes from each tree. Cut each sweet into three and place a piece in each hole. Make a hole at the top of each tree for threading the ribbon.

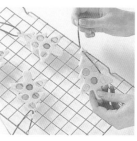

6 Bake for 15 minutes, until golden. Cool on the baking tray before transferring to wire racks and threading lengths of ribbon through the holes.

striped *cookies*

These multi-coloured cookies may be made in different flavours and colours and look wonderful tied in bundles or packed into gift boxes or jars. Eat them with vanilla ice cream or light desserts as a final touch to a Christmas feast.

MAKES 25

25G/1OZ WHITE CHOCOLATE

RED AND GREEN FOOD

   COLOURING DUSTS

2 EGG WHITES

90G/3½OZ/½ CUP SUGAR

50G/2OZ/½ CUP PLAIN

   (ALL-PURPOSE) FLOUR

50G/2OZ/¼ CUP UNSALTED

   BUTTER, MELTED

RIBBON, TO DECORATE

1 Preheat the oven to 190°C/375°F/Gas 5. Line two baking sheets with baking paper (parchment) and set aside.

2 Break up the white chocolate, place in a heatproof bowl over a saucepan of hot water, and stir until melted.

3 Divide the melted chocolate in half and add food colouring dust to each half to colour the chocolate red and green. Fill a piping bag with each colour and fold down the tops. Snip off the points.

4 Place the egg whites in a large bowl and whisk until stiff. Add the sugar gradually, whisking well after each addition, to make a thick meringue. Add the flour and melted butter and whisk until smooth. Drop four separate teaspoonfuls of the mixture on to the prepared baking sheets and spread evenly into thin rounds.

5 Pipe lines or zigzag patterns of green and red chocolate over each of the rounds.

6 Bake one sheet at a time for 3–4 minutes, until pale golden.

7 Loosen the cookies on the baking sheet with a palette knife (metal spatula) and return them to the oven for a few seconds to soften. Have four lightly oiled wooden spoon handles at hand.

8 Taking one cookie out of the oven at a time, roll it around an oiled wooden spoon handle and leave to set. Repeat with all of the remaining cookies.

9 When set, slip the cookies off the handles on to a wire rack.

10 Repeat with the remaining mixture and the red and green chocolate until all the mixture has been used, baking only one sheet of cookies at a time. If they are too hard to shape, simply return them to the oven for a few seconds to soften.

11 When the cookies are completely cool, tie them together with coloured ribbon, if you like, and pack into a glass jar or presentation box.

golden Christmas *tree*

You can decorate this stunning tree with any combination of candy, chocolate and gingerbread shapes, provided they are not too heavy. It can be used for a really impressive table centrepiece, trimmed with plenty of gold, or a brighter colour scheme.

MAKES 1 TREE

3 QUANTITIES GINGERBREAD
  DOUGH (SEE PAGE 38)

200G/7OZ ROYAL ICING (GLAZE)

GOLD DRAGEES

28CM/11IN ROUND GOLD
  CAKE BOARD

1 EMPTY 400G/14OZ CAN,
  WASHED

SELECTION OF GOLD-
  WRAPPED CANDY

1.5M/1½ YDS FINE GOLD
  BEADING

1.5M/1½ YDS FINE GOLD
  RIBBON

1 Preheat the oven to 180°/350°/Gas 4. Grease two baking sheets. Roll out one-third of the gingerbread dough and transfer to one of the baking sheets.

2 Cut out a 33 x 23cm/13 x 9in rectangle from the dough on the baking sheet. Cut in half lengthways to form two more rectangles. Cut one diagonally from corner to corner. Repeat with the second rectangle.

3 Roll out just under half of the remaining dough. Place on the other baking sheet and cut in to four more triangles.

4 Roll the remaining dough and cut out festive shapes. Cook in the oven, allowing about 8 minutes for the shapes and 15–20 minutes for the triangles.

5 Remove the cooked gingerbread from the oven and recut the diagonal lines. Leave to cool for 5 minutes, then transfer to a wire rack.

6 Put a third of the icing (glaze) into a piping bag and pipe small dots over each triangle. Secure gold dragées to the dots. Leave to set.

7 Put half of the remaining icing into a piping bag fitted with a star nozzle. Pipe a line of icing down the straight side and along the base of one triangle. Repeat on one other triangle. Do not leave to set.

8 Secure the straight sides of the triangles together on the cake board, so they meet at right angles. Rest the empty can over the top to hold them together. Add the remaining triangles, and leave to set.

9 Use more icing in the star nozzle to pipe rows of stars over the joins between the tree sections. Decorate the un-iced sides of each section with more gold dragées.

10 Using a writing nozzle, decorate the cookies. Leave to set.

11 Stick the cookies on by piping icing on to the tree and pressing them in place. Stick a star to the top of the tree. Stick the gold-wrapped candy between the cookies.

12 Put a dot of icing at the top of the tree and secure the gold beading. Trail it around the tree, securing with icing. Repeat with the ribbon. Leave to set.

festive *cookies*

These cookies are great fun to make as gifts. Any shape of cookie cutter can be used. Store the cookies in an airtight tin, and for a change, omit the lemon zest and add 25g/1oz/¼ cup of ground almonds and a few drops of almond essence (extract).

MAKES ABOUT 12

75G/3OZ/6 TBSP BUTTER

50G/2OZ/½ CUP ICING
(CONFECTIONER'S) SUGAR

GRATED ZEST OF 1 LEMON

1 EGG YOLK

175G/6OZ/1½ CUPS PLAIN
(ALL-PURPOSE) FLOUR

PINCH OF SALT

TO DECORATE

2 EGG YOLKS

RED AND GREEN FOOD
COLOURINGS

1 In a large bowl, beat the butter, sugar and lemon zest together until fluffy. Beat in the egg yolk and then sift in the flour and the salt. Knead to form a dough. Wrap in clear film (plastic wrap) and chill for 30 minutes.

2 Preheat the oven to 190°C/375°F/Gas 5. Lightly grease two large baking sheets On a lightly floured surface, roll out the dough thinly. Using a fluted cutter, stamp out as many cookies as you can.

3 Transfer the cookies on to the baking sheets. Mark the tops with a 2.5cm/1in holly leaf cutter and use a 5mm/¼in plain piping nozzle for the berries. Chill for about 10 minutes, until firm.

4 Meanwhile, put each egg yolk into a small cup. Mix red food colouring into one and green food colouring into the other. Using a small, clean paintbrush, paint the leaves and berries.

5 Bake the cookies for 10–12 minutes, or until they begin to colour around the edges. Let them cool slightly on the baking trays, and then transfer them to a wire rack to cool completely.

COOK'S TIP

When cooking with young children, things will flow more smoothly if you have all the ingredients to hand before they start to cook. Large aprons are a good idea for all involved.

If you prefer to start your Christmas baking in advance of the holiday season, you can freeze the cookies, either raw or baked. Don't forget to make a note of the baking time needed for raw cookies. Baked cookies that have been frozen will benefit from being refreshed in the oven after they have thawed.

Christmas *gingerbread*

In all its forms, gingerbread has been part of the Christmas tradition for generations. It is particularly well loved in Germany, from where many present-day gingerbread recipes originate.

MAKES 20

30ML/2 TBSP GOLDEN
   (LIGHT CORN) SYRUP

15ML/1 TBSP BLACK TREACLE
   (MOLASSES)

50G/2OZ/¼ CUP SOFT LIGHT
   BROWN SUGAR

25G/1OZ/2 TBSP BUTTER

175G/6OZ/1½ CUPS PLAIN
   (ALL-PURPOSE) FLOUR

3.5ML/¾ TSP BICARBONATE
   OF SODA (BAKING SODA)

2.5ML/½ TSP MIXED SPICE
   (ALL-SPICE)

7.5ML/1½ TSP GROUND
   GINGER

1 EGG YOLK

ICING AND DECORATION

90G/3½ OZ ROYAL ICING
   (GLAZE)

RED, YELLOW AND GREEN
   FOOD COLOURINGS

1M/1YD FESTIVE RIBBON

1 Preheat the oven to 190°C/375°F/ Gas 5. Line several baking sheets with baking paper (parchment). Place the syrup, treacle (molasses), sugar and butter in a pan. Heat gently, stirring, until the butter has melted.

2 Sift the flour, bicarbonate of soda (baking soda), mixed spice (all-spice) and ginger together in a mixing bowl. Using a wooden spoon, stir in the treacle mixture.

3 Add the egg yolk and mix to form a soft dough. Remove the dough from the bowl and knead on a lightly floured surface until smooth.

4 Roll out the dough thinly, and using a selection of festive cutters, such as stars and Christmas trees, stamp out the shapes, kneading and re-rolling the dough as necessary. Arrange the shapes, spaced apart, on the baking sheets.

5 Make a hole in the top of each shape, using a drinking straw, if you wish to use the cookies as decorations for the Christmas tree.

6 Bake in the oven for 15–20 minutes until firm and golden. Allow the cookies to cool on the baking sheets before transferring them to a wire rack to cool completely.

7 Divide the icing (glaze) into four and colour one quarter red, one quarter yellow and one quarter green, using the food colourings. Make four greaseproof (waxed) paper piping bags and fill each with a coloured icing. Fold down the tops and snip off the points.

8 Pipe lines, dots, and zigzags on the gingerbread cookies using the icings. Leave to dry. If you intend to hang the cookies, thread lengths of ribbon through the holes made earlier.

glazed ginger *cookies*

These tasty cookies are great to give to friends at Christmas, and they make perfect hanging decorations for trees and garlands. For this, make a hole in each cookie with a skewer, and thread with fine ribbon.

MAKES ABOUT 20

175G/6OZ/1½ CUPS PLAIN
   (ALL-PURPOSE) FLOUR
1.5ML/ ¼ TSP BICARBONATE
   OF SODA (BAKING SODA)
PINCH OF SALT
5ML/1 TSP GROUND GINGER
5ML/1 TSP GROUND
   CINNAMON
65G/2½ OZ/5 TBSP UNSALTED
   BUTTER, CHOPPED
75G/3OZ/SCANT ½ CUP
   SUGAR
30ML/2 TBSP GOLDEN
   (LIGHT CORN) SYRUP
1 EGG YOLK, BEATEN

ICING AND DECORATION

90G/3½OZ ROYAL ICING
   (GLAZE)
RED AND GREEN FOOD
   COLOURINGS
175G/6OZ WHITE ALMOND
   PASTE

1 To make the dough, sift together the flour, bicarbonate of soda (baking soda), salt and spices. Rub the butter into the flour, then add the sugar, syrup and egg yolk and mix to a firm dough. Knead lightly. Wrap in clear film (plastic wrap) and chill for 30 minutes.

2 Preheat the oven to 180°C/350°F/Gas 4. Grease a baking sheet. Roll out the dough on a floured surface and cut out a variety of shapes. Transfer to the baking sheet and bake for 8–10 minutes, until beginning to colour around the edges. Leave to rest for 3 minutes.

3 Transfer the cookies to a wire rack and leave to cool. Place the wire rack over a large tray or plate to catch any spills. Spoon the icing (glaze) over the cookies so that they are completely covered. Leave in a cool place to dry for 2–3 hours.

4 Knead red food colouring into half of the almond paste and green food colouring into the other half. Blend the colours in well.

5 Roll a thin length of each coloured paste and then twist the two together into a rope. Secure a rope of paste around each cookie, using small dots of the icing. Repeat on about half of the cookies.

6 Mix a little of the red and green food colourings separately with water. Using a fine paintbrush, paint festive decorations over the plain cookies. Leave to dry.

savoury *nibbles*

cocktail *shapes*

Savoury aperitif bites are always a welcome treat. Try different flavours and shapes for a more interesting gift.

MAKES 80

350G/12OZ/3 CUPS PLAIN
(ALL-PURPOSE) FLOUR

PINCH OF SALT

2.5ML/½ TSP BLACK PEPPER

5ML/1 TSP WHOLE GRAIN
MUSTARD

175G/6OZ/¾ CUP BUTTER,
CHOPPED

115G/4OZ CHEDDAR CHEESE

1 EGG, BEATEN

5ML/1 TSP CHOPPED NUTS

10ML/2 TSP DILL SEEDS

10ML/2 TSP CURRY PASTE

10ML/2 TSP CHILLI SAUCE

1 Preheat the oven to 200°C/400°F/Gas 6. Line several baking sheets with baking paper (parchment). Sift the flour into a bowl and add the salt, pepper and mustard.

2 Rub the butter into the flour mixture until it resembles fine breadcrumbs. Grate the cheese and stir it into the butter and flour mixture. Add the egg and mix to form a soft dough. Knead lightly on a floured surface and cut into four pieces.

3 Knead the nuts, dill seeds, curry paste and chilli sauce into each of the pieces. Wrap each piece in clear film (plastic wrap) and chill for at least 1 hour.

4 Remove from the clear film and roll out one piece at a time. Using a floured heart-shaped cutter, stamp out about 20 shapes from the curry-flavoured dough and use a club-shaped cutter for the chilli-flavoured dough.

5 Arrange the shapes well spaced apart on the baking sheets, and bake for 6–8 minutes, until slightly puffed and golden in colour. Cool on wire racks.

6 Repeat with the remaining flavoured dough using spade- and diamond-shaped cutters. Knead any trimmings together, re-roll and stamp out, and bake as above.

spicy *nibbles*

Shape these tasty cheese snacks in any way you wish – stars, crescent moons, triangles, squares, hearts, fingers or rounds. Delicious served with drinks, whether ice-cold cocktails or hot and spicy mulls.

MAKES 60

115G/4OZ/1 CUP PLAIN
(ALL-PURPOSE) FLOUR,
PLUS EXTRA FOR DUSTING
5ML/1 TSP MUSTARD POWDER
PINCH OF SALT
115G/4OZ/½ CUP BUTTER
75G/3OZ/¾ CUP CHEDDAR
CHEESE, GRATED
PINCH OF CAYENNE PEPPER

30ML/2 TBSP WATER
1 EGG, BEATEN
POPPY SEEDS, SUNFLOWER
SEEDS OR SESAME SEEDS,
TO DECORATE

1 Preheat the oven to 200°C/400°F/Gas 6. Lightly grease two baking sheets and set them aside.

2 Sift the flour, mustard powder and salt into a bowl and rub in the butter until the mixture resembles breadcrumbs. Stir in the cheese and pepper and sprinkle on the water. Add half the egg, mix to a dough and knead until smooth.

3 Roll out the dough on a floured surface and cut out shapes.

4 Place on the baking sheets and brush with the remaining egg. Sprinkle on the seeds. Bake for 8–10 minutes until golden.

cheese *straws*

MAKES 50 STRAWS AND
8 RINGS

115G/4OZ/1 CUP PLAIN
(ALL-PURPOSE) FLOUR,
PLUS EXTRA FOR
DUSTING
5ML/1 TSP MUSTARD
POWDER
PINCH OF SALT

115G/4OZ/½ CUP BUTTER
75G/3OZ/¾ CUP CHEDDAR
CHEESE, GRATED
PINCH OF CAYENNE PEPPER
30ML/2 TBSP WATER

1 Preheat the oven to 200°C/400°F/Gas 6. Grease two baking sheets.

2 Make the pastry in the same way as Spicy Nibbles. Cut the pastry into 10cm/4in x 5mm/¼in fingers.

3 Dust the work surface with flour and roll out the trimmings.

4 Use a 6cm/2½in diameter cutter to cut the circle and a 5cm/2in diameter cutter to cut the centre. Brush with the remaining egg and bake for 8 minutes. To serve, push six cheese straws through each ring.

thyme and mustard *cookies*

These aromatic cookies are delicious served with herby cheese as a savoury ending to a light summer lunch.

MAKES 40

175G/6OZ/1½ CUPS
WHOLEMEAL PLAIN
(ALL-PURPOSE) FLOUR

50G/2OZ/½ CUP OATMEAL

25G/1OZ/2 TBSP SUGAR

10ML/2 TSP BAKING POWDER

30ML/2 TBSP FRESH THYME
LEAVES

50G/2OZ/¼ CUP BUTTER,
CHOPPED

25G/1OZ/2 TBSP WHITE
VEGETABLE FAT
(SHORTENING), CHOPPED

45ML/3 TBSP MILK

10ML/2 TSP DIJON MUSTARD

30ML/2 TBSP SESAME SEEDS

SALT AND BLACK PEPPER

1 Preheat the oven to 200°C/400°F/ Gas 6. Grease two baking sheets and set aside.

2 Put the dry ingredients, thyme leaves and seasoning into a bowl and mix. Add the fats, then rub in.

3 Mix the milk and mustard together and stir into the flour mixture to make a soft dough.

4 Knead on a floured surface then roll out thinly. Stamp out rounds with a floured cookie cutter, and arrange on the prepared baking sheets.

5 Roll the trimmings and stamp out more cookies until the dough is used. Prick the cookies with a fork and sprinkle with sesame seeds.

6 Cook for 10 minutes, until lightly browned. Cool on the sheets then pack into a small airtight container. Store in a cool place for up to 5 days.

savoury cocktail *cookies*

Serve these savoury cookies at a party or with pre-dinner drinks. Each of the spice seeds contributes to the flavour.

MAKES 20–30

150G/5OZ/1¼ CUPS PLAIN
   (ALL-PURPOSE) FLOUR

10ML/2 TSP CURRY POWDER

115G/4OZ/½ CUP BUTTER,
   CHOPPED

75G/3OZ/¾ CUP GRATED
   CHEDDAR CHEESE

10ML/2 TSP POPPY SEEDS

5ML/1 TSP BLACK ONION
   SEEDS

1 EGG YOLK

CUMIN SEEDS, TO GARNISH

VARIATION

Try using caraway or sesame seeds in place of the poppy seeds, if you wish.

1 Grease two baking sheets. Sift the flour and curry powder into a large mixing bowl.

2 Rub in the butter until the mixture resembles breadcrumbs.

3 Stir in the cheese, poppy seeds, black onion seeds and egg yolk, and mix to a firm dough. Wrap in clear film (plastic wrap) and chill for 30 minutes.

4 Dust a rolling pin and roll out the dough on a floured surface to a thickness of about 3mm/⅛in.

5 Cut into rounds with a floured cutter. Arrange on the prepared baking sheets and sprinkle with the cumin seeds. Chill for 15 minutes.

6 Preheat the oven to 190°C/375°F/Gas 5. Bake for 20 minutes, until the cookies are crisp and golden. Cool slightly and serve warm or cold.

peanut *cookies*

The combinaton of salt and sweet flavours is truly delicious.

MAKES 70

350G/12OZ/3 CUPS PLAIN
(ALL-PURPOSE) FLOUR

2.5ML/½ TSP BICARBONATE
OF SODA (BAKING SODA)

115G/4OZ/½ CUP BUTTER

115G/4OZ/½ CUP MARGARINE

250G/9OZ/1¼ CUPS LIGHT
BROWN SUGAR

2 EGGS

10ML/2 TSP VANILLA ESSENCE
(EXTRACT)

225G/8OZ/2 CUPS SALTED
PEANUTS

1 Preheat the oven to 190°C/375°F/Gas 5. Grease two baking sheets. Mix the flour and bicarbonate of soda (baking soda).

2 With an electric mixer, cream the butter, margarine and sugar. Beat in the eggs and vanilla. Fold in the flour mixture.

3 Stir the peanuts into the butter mixture until evenly combined. Drop teaspoonfuls 5cm/2in apart on the prepared sheets. Grease the bottom of a glass and dip in sugar, and use this to flatten the cookies. Bake for 10 minutes, until lightly coloured. Transfer to a wire rack to cool.

Cheddar *pennies*

For a gift, pack these tasty cheese snacks into an airtight tin.

MAKES 20

50G/2OZ/¼ CUP BUTTER

115G/4OZ/1 CUP CHEDDAR
CHEESE, GRATED

40G/1½OZ/⅓ CUP PLAIN
(ALL-PURPOSE) FLOUR

PINCH OF SALT

PINCH OF CHILLI POWDER

1 Using an electric mixer, blend the butter until soft and creamy. Stir in the cheese, flour, salt and chilli powder. Gather to form a dough, then turn out on to a lightly floured surface.

2 Shape the dough into a cylinder about 3cm/1¼in in diameter. Wrap in greaseproof (waxed) paper and chill for 1–2 hours.

3 Preheat the oven to 180°C/350°F/Gas 4. Grease two baking sheets.

4 Cut into 20 slices and place on the baking sheets. Bake for 15 minutes. Leave to cool.

index